CONCEPTUAL ILLUSTRATION

GENERAL ILLUSTRATION

HUMOR

LETTERING DESIGN

Introductory essay by Philip Smith

Portfolios derived from N.Y.GOLD Volume 3.

N.Y.GOLD

CONCEPTUAL ILLUSTRATION

INDEX

GENERAL ILLUSTRATION
HUMOR
LETTERING DESIGN

PORTFOLIO INDEX

General Illustration

Illustrators & *Representatives*

Humorous Illustration

Illustrators & *Representatives*

Lettering & Design

Letterers/Designers

CONCEPTUAL ILLUSTRATION

Phillip Smith

BY ITS VERY NATURE, conceptual illustration combines the best of art and ideas. What results in this very special type of illustration are images that stop the eye and start the mind. The images collected in this book are not just straight product shots or portraits. Instead they are pictures in which "something happens." Conceptual illustration is loaded with thoughtful emotions and expressive messages. The images take you "somewhere else" away from the printed page into another realm of appreciation. Above all, they are images primarily concerned with communication.

CONCEPTUAL ILLUSTRATION FUNCTIONS not only as a portfolio of some of today's most talented illustrators, but also as an idea book rich in provocative imagery. Throughout its contents are illustrations ranging from witty one-liners to psychologically probing pictures. Their unique connecting thread is that the images in this book function as high voltage communicators. These illustrations are so well conceived that they are capable of expressing the contents of an entire annual report in a single picture. Above all, this book allows you to see the artist's thinking at work. Both their conceptual and technical solutions are visible in each of the illustrations contained in these pages.

WE HOPE ILLUSTRATORS, editors and art directors will constantly refer to this volume, not only for talent but also for inspiration. *Conceptual Illustration* is a source of some of the most innovative ideas currently being produced in illustration today. The work offers a wide range of visual solutions to communications problems encountered by corporations, graphic design firms, magazines and advertising agencies.

EACH OF THESE images represents a solution to a problem posed by a client. "How do we represent what our company does?" "How can we re-position ourselves?" "How do you editorially convey the problems of too much salt in the diet?" "How do you make the point concerning hostile takeovers in the corporate world?" In this book we see the work of a very special breed of illustrators. True, they must be technically brilliant and able to create recognizeable images. But above all they must be able to translate a client's issue into highly effective and informative illustrations.

EVERY ILLUSTRATOR APPROACHES an assignment in a unique way. Some listen, take notes and go away to quietly search for a solution. Sketch after sketch is created until an answer presents itself. Other engage the art director in an intensive

© Steve Dininno

dialogue to pierce the heart of the issue needing to be portrayed. Finally, there are the few lucky ones who are able to get the concept firmly fixed in their minds during the initial conversation with the art director. For them it is a matter of a tight presentation sketch and off to work they go.

MANY OF THE ILLUSTRATORS featured in this book owe some form of debt to the art of surrealism. Creating psychologically loaded images that transcend reality was part of the underlying principle of surrealism. Juxtaposing different fragments of reality allows the artist to suspend belief, and thereby experience a new form of perception.

THE ILLUSTRATOR IS FREE to create images not found in daily life. For example, Steve Dininno (on page 37) fabricates surreal landscapes in which music listeners hover in the sky on U.F.O.'s made from compact disks. Or in another image he creates a depositor waiting in front of a bank with his piggy bank tied to an American flag hitching post. It each case he creates a para-normal world in which the imagination rules and experienced reality fades.

TWO ARTISTS, IN PARTICULAR, have developed their own unique vision based partly on the work of surrealist painter Rene Magritte. Jean-Francois Podevin produces masterful painterly illustrations with a visually intellectual slant. On page 40 we see a well-dressed gentleman whose face is composed of a set of eye glasses and two other supporting gentlemen. All of this set within a frame within a frame. The image gives us enormous pause, opening both our intellect and our eyes. Rendering each of the elements in a highly realistic style with almost photographic quality adds the power of believeability to Podevin's work.

© Jean-Francois Podevin

ON THE OTHER HAND, Robert Goldstrom utilizes surrealism with a lighter touch. On page 9 we see an illustration created for Macmillan Publishing of a man shaving. As he does so, he reveals the sky and clouds behind him. Goldstrom utilizes a

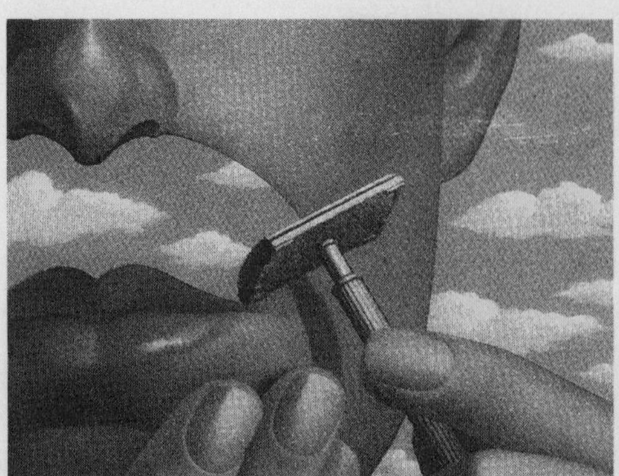

© Robert Goldstrom

bag of mental tricks that makes us experience with a tickled mind.

Bob Peters has a playful touch when he alters reality. On page 43 we see his Champion spark plug poised for a power lift-off like a Saturn rocket. Also on the same page, Peters has created a meaningful image of a blissful natural paradise just beneath the surface of a spoiled landscape. With wishful fantasy he turns the everyday world topsy-turvey into a land where anything is possible. It is these vast leaps of imagination that give so much of the visual power to conceptual illustration.

Conceptual illustration presents not only a wealth of illustration concepts and styles, but of techniques as well. While many of the illustrators use traditional materials, such as oil paint or watercolor, others utilize unorthodox combinations of transparent films, transfer lettering and photocopies. A number of illustrators have invented their own techniques as required to express their particular concepts. Whatever their method, these illustrators are an important link in the creative chain. More than an art director's alter ego, conceptual illustrators serve as Mr. Wizards to an art director's needs. From their paints and pencils, they conjure up magical and imaginative imagery.

© Bob Peters

Unlike traditional assignments, where the final illustration is guided and shaped by the art director, the look and content of the images in this book are the responsibility of the conceptual illustrator. These days, more often than not, the art director presents a problem rather than a solution to the conceptual illustrator. Many of the illustrators featured here state that the art director gave them a word or a sentence and said, "You go figure it out." This may seem like lazy art direction, but it puts the illustrator's mind into high gear. Possibly too much direction is a handicap for the artist's imaginative wanderings. After all, visual thinking is their specialty. For example, when Warren Gebert received a call from TIME Inc., he was given the assignment with a brief word, "Creativity." This was enough to start the wheels turning. Gebert visualized surviving a flood by inverting an umbrella into a life raft and thereby safely navigating the storm (page 14).

Advertising and editorial clients love conceptual illustration for the simple reason that

© E.H. Smith

it grabs you. It's that "something more," that psychological twist in the illustration, that makes you think as well as look. In a sense, the client gets more for his or her money, because the viewers and readers spend more time engaged with the picture. This of course means more time selling the product or capturing the reader's interest.

A SPECIAL SECTION of this book has been devoted to humorous illustration. The imagery ranges from the slapstick, prankster approach of Elwood H. Smith (page 47), to the perfectly mixed martini dry wit of Tim Lewis (page 53). Unless properly conceived, humor can fall flat on its face. Mind you, these illustrations are not to be confused with cartoons. They are a separate breed unto themselves.

© Tim Lewis

HUMOR IS ANOTHER WAY of getting the message across. Its impact tends to be immediate. Humor hits the guts first and the mind second. Art directors wisely use humor to handle delicate situations. Humor is a "friendly sell" and can often diffuse tough issues of finance, liability global politics or product representation. Humor can be very seductive, it operates when your defenses are down. How can you not like humor? In the right situation, humor as a vehicle for selling products or ideas can't be beat.

THE HUMORIST, LIKE the conceptual illustrator, has to conceive the illustration on a number of levels. First of all the client's message must come through loud and clear. Secondly, the humor must be appropriate to the situation and widely understood. The humor illustrations represented in this book encompass a great deal of fantasy as well as whimsy. They range from the caricature style of Steve Haefele (page 63) to the adult comic strips of Bonnie Timmons (page 59). But above all, each one of the illustrators has his or her own standards of sophistication. It's a healthy sign that the culture is alive and well by the growing number of humorists.

FOR THE ILLUSTRATOR, *CONCEPTUAL ILLUSTRATION* should serve not only as an idea book, but also as a behind-the-scenes look at some of the best illustration in the business. To this end we have profiled a number of illustrators, discussing how they arrive at their unique solutions, their inter-actions with art directors, and how they illustrate their concepts. Like their work, each illustrator approaches an assignment with a unique vision and style. The development of each image in this book has required brainstorming, sketching, revisions and finally execution.

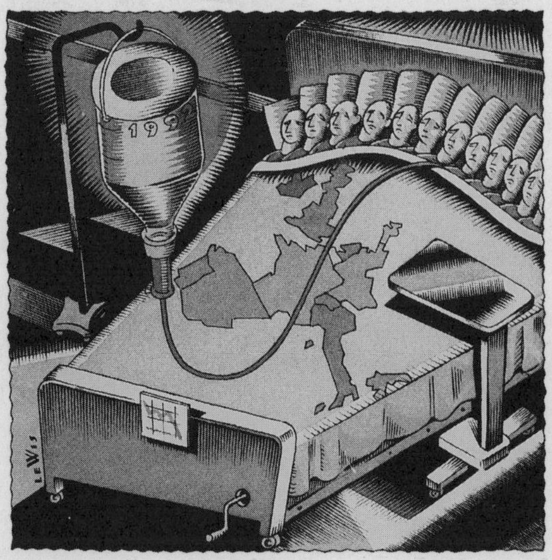

© Tim Lewis

WE HOPE *CONCEPTUAL ILLUSTRATION* with its profiles of the artists and its collection of imaginative imagery will enlighten you with some of the most exceptional examples of the art of illustration.

CASE STUDY

David Lesh

In his illustration work, David Lesh uses a variety of media to get his point across. Oil pastel, photography, colored pencils, transfer lettering, photocopies and oil paint are a few of the materials used to create his painting-like conceptual illustrations. In each piece, Lesh combines a number of unrelated elements in a collage-like fashion to create a singular visual statement (see pages 24–25).

Lesh feels that his work is different from other types of illustration and that it communicates on a unique level. He explains, "People are attracted to my work, because it makes a statement not available with a conventional photograph. I like to create visual statements in an off-the-wall way." For Lesh, assignments provide an opportunity to stretch his thinking and explore a range of visual possibilities.

Because so many of Lesh's clients are long-distance ones, he has learned to refine his thinking and presentation techniques. Lesh feels that "90% of what I do is based on one sentence from the art director." With this bit of information, he begins to do "tons of thumbnails until I hit on a solution." In these thumbnails Lesh explores a range of problem-solving concepts that he feels will best serve the client. Once he feels comfortable with one of the sketches, it is then turned into a tighter sketch with a tissue overlay. The overlay provides the art director with a commentary of the piece, explaining not only colors and media to be used, but more importantly the significance of each image and how it pertains to the client's particular problem. Each of these sketches is accompanied by a booklet of Lesh's work that will provide the art director with a more thorough understanding of Lesh's technique and style. Usually at this point the project is a go.

Recently, Lesh received a phone call from art director David Bloch in Manhattan. He needed a cover illustration for the annual report of Republic Bank. The topic was "Risk in Banking." Lesh's piece had to express the concept of "minimal risk."

Lesh began his brainstorming, sketching process. After looking at a variety of solutions, he liked the idea of a tightrope walker, but with a safety net or at least being close to the ground. This would express both minimal risk and balance. This was then tightened up into a line drawing with a tissue overlay explaining the look and direction of the piece. It is at this point that any changes in the illustration must be made. Once Lesh begins the final creative process, alterations become impossible.

The sketch was sent via overnight mail to art director Bloch for his review. He liked the piece. Lesh had included the word "risk" in the sketch. After a brief dis-

© David Lesh

cussion, it was eliminated, and Lesh was given the green light.

To begin the illustration process, Lesh hired a model and photographed him in a variety of tightrope-walking poses. He processed the film in his own lab in the studio. The man was then sized down and photocopied, so that he could be hand-colored. The supporting profile that he is tightroping across came from Lesh's picture file. A dollar bill used to indicate the concept of "banking" was photocopied and then cutout in the shape of the profile. As with the man, the dollar bill was hand-colored.

Lesh then began assembling the various elements on a 12″ × 15″ illustration board. The next step was the coloring of the background with various media. The multi-colored safety net in the profile's head was done with stripes of Prisma color. The signature white background that Lesh has become known for is done with oil paint. The various colored highlights in the piece were created with "whatever materials are handy," which in this case included oil pastel. Finishing graphic touches such as the arrows, circles and lettering were done with rubber stamps, pen and ink and transfer lettering.

The finished illustration took Lesh approximately a week. He then photographed the piece in his studio onto a 4″ × 5″ transparency. "I never send the original. With the correct lighting, I can highlight the texture and in some way control the final reproduction. In this case the piece was printed on an uncoated stock and tipped into a debossed area on the cover of the annual report. They handled my work with great care and respect. I was very pleased with the final results." Lesh describes the cover for the Republic Bank as "a great job. There were few changes, and the final outcome was terrific."

Lesh points out that he "doesn't use found images, and I don't just retouch photographs." Because of the amount of work and thinking that goes into each of Lesh's illustrations, he chooses clients and assignments as carefully as they choose him. "If I am asked to just put some gesso around a photograph of some guys in a board room, I'm not interested. But if the assignment challenges me and allows me to take the project to a new level, then we can talk."

CASE STUDY

Warren Gebert

Warren Gebert, is a real problem solver (see pages 14–15). When he gets an assignment, he just sits down and thinks. Maybe he'll watch TV or make a list of words that illustrate the idea. But before he starts a sketch, he has the idea firmly planted in his mind.

When TIME Inc. called Gebert for an assignment, the art director Kent Hunter was not very forthcoming with a direction. Several artists were being chosen to illustrate the interior of TIME's annual report. Each of the artists was given a word to illustrate. Gebert's word was "Creativity". When he pressed the art director for a bit more information, Hunter explained that the theme of this section was managing a corporate division with flexibility and creativity. Gebert inquired as to who the other illustrators were. This gave him a sense of whether or not the annual report was going to be conservative or somewhat adventurous.

During that talk on the phone, the solution came to Gebert. He started with the concept of an umbrella. In the middle of a flood, an umbrella is of little or no use. Therefore, rethink your tools and your umbrella can become a life saving boat. He saw this solution as an appropriate message to managers. It captured the essence of enlightened corporate leadership.

After the phone call Gebert sat down to sketch out his vision. He refined the idea and came up with four additional proposals. The sketches were then faxed over to Hunter. He liked all of them and told Gebert to pursue whichever one he enjoyed the most. Gebert, like many artists, chose his initial idea. Hunter's only comment was to make sure that the guy in the boat had on a suit of a different color to distinguish him from the others.

Once he gets the go ahead, Gebert doesn't like sketches sitting around waiting to be developed into final paintings. He gets right into the project, usually finishing it overnight.

Most of Gebert's illustrations are done on 3-ply Bristol paper with acrylic paint. First, he sizes out the sketch onto the paper and gets a general idea of placement and colors. Then he proceeds to paint in the scene, whether it is a landscape or an interior without the people. This method allows him to get a better sense of how the humans will interact with their environment. The people are added, followed by shadows and highlights.

© Warren Gebert

When Gebert presented the finished painting to the art director, he wanted the horizon line brightened a bit to indicate a more optimistic direction for the painting. Gebert had no problem with this suggestion and complied.

Part of the strength of Gebert's work is due to his moody palette and tone, which expresses human challenges. It is exactly this sensibility that makes his work so ideal for art directors who need to get a complex message across. Whether seen in a commercial or editorial context, the illustrations express in a thoughtful, yet off-beat, fashion the dilemmas faced by modern men and women.

Gebert does no picture research for his assignments. He makes up all of his own imagery. In this way, he feels better able to communicate an idea, rather than getting caught up in the exactitude of what something is supposed to look like. This allows him a greater range of expression.

CASE STUDY

Tim Lewis

"I am not a decorative humorous illustrator," says Tim Lewis. "Nor is my work cartoony. I think I interject a sophisticated attitude into my work, a bit like the old Vanity Fair" (see page 53).

Lewis began his career some time ago at New York's Pushpin studios. "There was a witty attitude around the studio, and I plugged into that. As my career developed I noticed a growing sophistication among art directors. They became more willing to utilize illustrations with a more stylized point of view." Lewis claims that when he is presented with an assignment, the solution invariably contains elements of light-hearted wit. "I'm not much for grim, dark images."

His entertaining solutions were a natural for a recent issue of Warner Communications in-house quarterly magazine designed by Pentagram. Art director Harold Burch needed an image illustrating the growing impact of compact disks over traditional long-playing records. Warner, it seems, has an enormous list of musical artists on C.D.'s and is making an all-out effort to promote them. Lewis was simply given the facts about the new presence of C.D.'s in the marketplace and was told to take it from there.

Much of Lewis's style is due to the classic lines of Art Deco from the twenties. His conceptual thinking seems to echo his drawing style. He prefers, whenever possible, to have at least a week to mull over solutions to illustration problems. Finally, he came up with four or five ideas that included a C.D. and an L.P. slugging it out in a boxing ring, a C.D. and an L.P. on a seesaw and the final version of the musical formats as David and Goliath.

Lewis then began to produce his concept sketches for submission. All of his sketches are done with a Rolling Writer marker pen on 8½″ × 11″ typewriter paper. The slightly rough edge of the paper provides a slightly uneven line quality that he considers part of his "look." With each of the concepts now worked out in black and white, he sent them off to Harold Burch for final selection.

The image of the C.D. attacking the L.P. with a musical note won Burch's approval hands down. The art director did suggest some minor changes that included dressing David in a new costume. Burch then gave Lewis the go-ahead to proceed to final art.

With the OK, Lewis began to redraw the illustration once more onto typewriter paper with his favorite Rolling Writer pen. In

© Tim Lewis

this version, he makes whatever corrections were indicated by the art director. David was quickly recostumed into shorts and a leather tunic. All final decisions about image size and placement are made at this point. "This black-and-white sketch is crucial for me. The drawing has to work in its black-and-white format. If it doesn't, the addition of color is not going to save the illustration."

Lewis takes this drawing over to the copy shop and has it photo-copied onto 90-lb English watercolor paper. He always makes a number of copies of the original drawing to work from. This unusual technique gives him the freedom to experiment with a variety of color palettes without the laborious task of redrawing his image over and over again.

Onto these photo-copied templates, Lewis applies watercolor washes for coloration. With a stack of these photo-copied drawings, Lewis can explore a variety of color strategies. "This photocopying technique allows me to be much more adventurous with color." The result is an illustration that appears to imitate wood engravings or scratchboard.

Lewis strongly feels that various color versions create very different final illustrations. He usually provides the art director with a selection of two or three images in different color options. According to Lewis, the art directors appreciate the opportunity of having the choice.

The piece was reproduced a bit smaller than the original. Interestingly, the illustration was spotted by a German publisher. They requested usage for their corporate magazine, titled "Manager". Because Lewis had granted Warner Communications first North American rights, he was free to resell the image. Lewis was enormously pleased because it demonstrated that his work is able to transcend both cultural and language barriers.

CASE STUDY

Rafal Olbinski

Throughout Rafal Olbinski's work, one is aware of a classical training and sensibility. His illustrations are permeated with an understanding of the grand tradition of European surrealism. The often incongruous mixture of symbolic elements neatly fuse to give the images their sense of deeper meaning (see page 33).

© Rafal Olbinski

Solutions come to Olbinski through slow and deliberate thinking. Problems presented to him by an art director require thoughtful sketching and analysis. After a meeting with various members of the Bowne Corporation discussing their goals of international expansion, Olbinski went home to think and sketch. It was up to him to interpret their figures and projections and produce a significant image. His assignment was to illustrate Bowne's forthcoming annual report. Bowne is a financial printer that produces a wealth of financial documents, including stocks and securities.

Olbinski's sketches are always very rough. "Basically, they are just concepts with no real indication of design or color decisions. For this particular project, I produced five or six freehand drawings. From the meeting with the various members of Bowne, I began to think of this image of birds flying around the world as they spoke of their plans for global expansion."

Adding a surrealistic twist onto this concept, the birds became flying documents. Representation of Bowne's international scope was portrayed in the clouds shaped as the various continents. Olbinski rarely uses any reference in his sketch-

© Rafal Olbinski

ing or painting. In this particular assignment, he did consult an atlas to provide general accuracy for the "cloud map."

"Once the art director has approved the idea and made his comments, I never do another sketch. Instead, I start painting immediately. The final result is often surprising, not only to myself, but to the art director as well." The painting for this particular illustration was produced with acrylics on masonite board. Olbinski prefers the speed with which acrylics dry, enabling him to create a painting within two or three days.

"When I present the finished painting to the art director, they very rarely make any suggestions or changes." Surely, this indicates the best of all qualities in a conceptual illustrator—that of being a mind reader and magician.

Conceptual illustration must be able to speak a multitude of languages and meanings to as many different audiences. Therein lies one of the delicate balancing acts the illustrator has to achieve. Making sure that the image communicates over and over again to a broad audience is no easy task. This requires multilevel thinking on the part of the artist. To insure that the client's concerns and the artistic integrity of the piece are combined with the desires of the audience, the artist must first start with a sound concept refined into a straight arrow heading towards its target. For this reason, the artists shown here have earned the title of conceptual illustrators.

© Rafal, Olbinski

Above all, conceptual illustration is a unique selling tool. As companies continue to aim at the growing, upscale audience, they must approach people through ever-increasing methods of visual sophistication. Agencies and corporations alike have finally recognized that the American public is not only awake and alive, but also more intelligent and sophisticated. Advertising images must therefore appeal to their aesthetics as well as tease their minds. Images projected at this audience must create not only with an awareness of the product or company, but with a satisfying memorable experience as well.

The existence of this book indicates the increasing maturation of the American audience and the type of information it requires. We have become Europeanized and are interested not only in well-designed products but a life that matches as well. In short, the artists collected in this volume represent the internationalization of American thinking. Whether it is the forties look of John Howard (page 8) with his post-depression romanticism or the technical wizardry of Terry Allen's pinball-like figures (page 36), *Conceptual Illustration* exhibits a superlative range of some of the best visual thinking this country has to offer.

CASE STUDY

Robert Pizzo

Robert Pizzo has been strongly influenced by the highly graphic posters of the depression era W.P.A. His black and white illustrations have a jazz age sensibility to them. When color is applied, the imagery becomes a bit more pop oriented. Whenever Pizzo takes on an assignment, the solutions are always filtered through his stylized, machine-age aesthetic (see pages 12–13).

"I'm a one-sketch man. It's always worked for me," says Pizzo. "Usually an idea pops into my head as I'm talking to the art director. However, a lot of this depends upon how well the art director is communicating his needs to me. Some of my other friends produce a lot of sketches before they come up with a solution. Not me. First I tell the art director what I want to do. Usually I get an OK at that point. I won't show an art director a sketch until it's 100% perfect. This tight sketch helps both of us to visualize what's going on.

"Some time ago I sent the art director at Huffy a black-and-white mailer of my work. He seemed to like it." The Huffy Corporation is mainly known for its line of quality bicycles. Now, they have diversified and manufacture such products as basketballs and monitors for children. For their annual report they needed a cover that represented the diversity of the company. "The art director gave me a series of quotes from various division managers that were to appear in the annual report. Each of these managers talked about their particular part of the company.

"The first thought that came to me is that they needed a positive image. Something that tied the whole company together. I hit on this image of a worker guy holding up a bike and all the movement and energy radiating outward from him. I knew that I could be fairly abstract in my representations."

Pizzo faxed a "100% perfect" tight sketch to the art director. The only change was to alter the bicycle. Pizzo's depiction was of a racing bike with an elongated seat and turned down handlebars. The art director wanted something that looked more like a mountain bike. Pizzo made the requested corrections.

To begin the final illustration, Pizzo photocopies his sketch. Over this he lays a piece of vellum and begins to ink-in the lines and black areas with a marker. Patterns and textures are created with Letraset film patterns. If color is needed, it is added with Pantone colored film. This vellum is then sent to the art director as the finished art to be shot for their needs.

The black-and-white illustration was used on the cover of the Huffy annual report. The art director consulted with Pizzo to make appropriate selections of background color and supporting type. In addition, Pizzo was commissioned to create five additional illustrations for the report's interior. "The art director let me do the kind of work I do best and consulted with me on my color and type preferences. That meant a lot to me. Sometimes an art director combines my work with an awful piece of type, and it just kills the whole thing. Huffy was a great client."

ILLUSTRATION

R O B E R T   G I U S T I

340 LONG MOUNTAIN ROAD
NEW MILFORD, CONNECTICUT 06776
(203) 354-6539

Represented By:
MILTON NEWBORN ASSOCIATES
135 EAST 54TH STREET
NEW YORK, NEW YORK 10022
(212) 421-0050   FAX (212) 421-0444

NIXDORF COMPUTER

ATLANTIC MONTHLY

SUNTORY CO

M A R K   H E S S

88 QUICKS LANE
KATONAH, NEW YORK 10536
(914) 232-5870

Represented By:
MILTON NEWBORN ASSOCIATES
135 EAST 54TH STREET
NEW YORK, NEW YORK 10022
(212) 421-0050   FAX (212) 421-0444

BACARDI RUM

U.S. POSTAL SERVICE

U.S. FIDELITY & GUARANTY

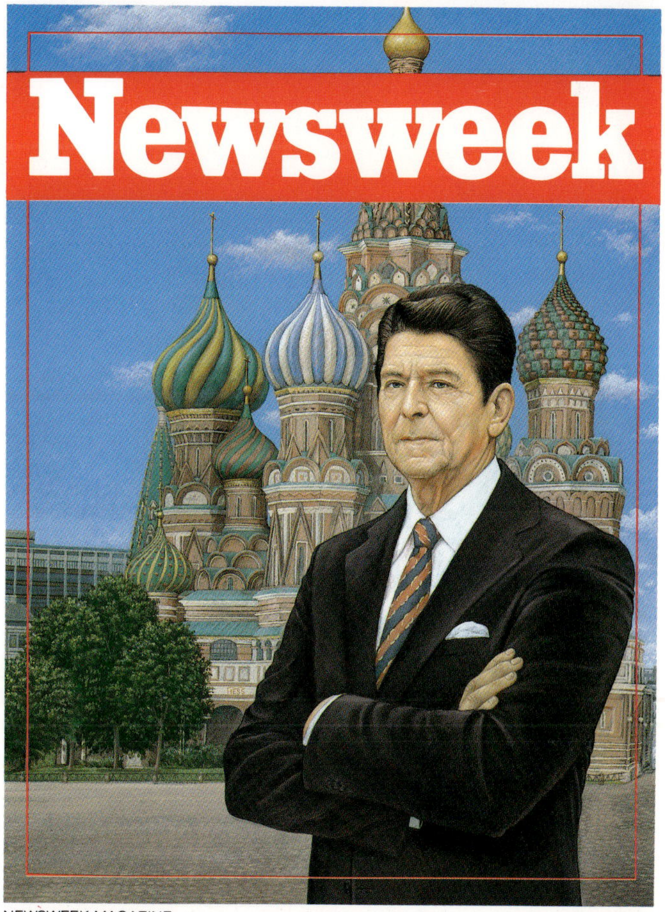

NEWSWEEK MAGAZINE

VICTOR JUHASZ

576 WESTMINSTER AVENUE
ELIZABETH, NEW JERSEY 07208
(201) 351-4227

Represented By:
MILTON NEWBORN ASSOCIATES
135 EAST 54TH STREET
NEW YORK, NEW YORK 10022
(212) 421-0050   FAX (212) 421-0444

NIXDORF COMPUTER

OXFORD UNIVERSITY PRESS

D A V I D   W I L C O X

5955 SAWMILL ROAD
DOYLESTOWN, PENNSYLVANIA 18901
(215) 297-0849

Represented By:
MILTON NEWBORN ASSOCIATES
135 EAST 54TH STREET
NEW YORK NEW YORK 10022
(212) 421-0050 FAX (212) 421-0444

3 COM

MERRILL LYNCH & CO

R I C H A R D   H E S S

310 LITCHFIELD ROAD
NORFOLK, CONNECTICUT 06058
(203) 542-5529

Represented By:
MILTON NEWBORN ASSOCIATES
135 EAST 54TH STREET
NEW YORK, NEW YORK 10022
(212) 421-0050 FAX (212) 421-0444

TIME MAGAZINE

GENERAL RE

GENERAL RE

119 WYKEHAM ROAD
WASHINGTON, CONNECTICUT 06793
(203) 868-7577

Represented By:
MILTON NEWBORN ASSOCIATES
135 EAST 54TH STREET
NEW YORK, NEW YORK 10022
(212) 421-0050 FAX (212) 421-0444

NEWSWEEK

NIXDORF COMPUTER

R.R. DONELLEY & SONS

BALLANTINE BOOKS

NEW AMERICAN LIBRARY

C.B.S. RECORDS

FIRST INTERSTATE BANK

JOHN H. HOWARD

(212) 832-7980

represented by

JOAN SIGMAN

TEL: (212) 421-0050 336 E. 54TH. ST., N.Y.C. 10022 FAX: (212) 421-0444

CHAMPION INTERNATIONAL

MACMILLAN PUBLISHING

DOUBLEDAY PUBLISHING

DOUBLEDAY PUBLISHING

ROBERT GOLDSTROM

(718) 768-7367

represented by

JOAN SIGMAN

TEL: (212) 421-0050 336 E. 54TH ST., N.Y.C. 10022 FAX: (212) 421-0444

DAVID MONTIEL

115 WEST 16TH STREET APT 211
NEW YORK CITY
10011

212-929-3659
718-788-6118

TOM CURRY
302 LAKEHILLS DRIVE
AUSTIN, TEXAS 78733
(512) 263-3407
FAX (512) 263-3705

Represented in New York by:
EILEEN MOSS
333 EAST 49th ST.
NEW YORK, NEW YORK 10017
(212) 980-8061

RANDOM HOUSE, 'The Messiah of Stockholm'

GSB CHICAGO, 'Hostile Takeovers'

WARNER LAMBERT, Annual Report

ROBERT PIZZO 288 E. DEVONIA AVE. MT. VERNON, N.Y. 10552 **914-664-4423**

R E P R E S E N T E D B Y

EILEEN MOSS & ASSOC. 333 E. 49TH ST. N.Y. N.Y. 10017 **212-980-8061**

[FOR EDITORIAL ASSIGNMENTS PLEASE CALL ROBERT DIRECTLY]

Huffy Corporation Annual Report
▸A Dedication to Service

1988

ROBERT PIZZO 288 E. DEVONIA AVE. MT. VERNON, N.Y. 10552 **914-664-4423**
R E P R E S E N T E D B Y
EILEEN MOSS & ASSOC. 333 E.49TH ST. N.Y. N.Y. 10017 **212-980-8061**
[FOR EDITORIAL ASSIGNMENTS PLEASE CALL ROBERT DIRECTLY]

WARREN GEBERT • 12 STONEHAM LANE NEW CITY, N.Y. 10956 914-354-2536
R E P R E S E N T E D B Y
EILEEN MOSS & ASSOC. • 333 E. 49TH ST. N.Y. N.Y. 10017 212-980-8061
FOR EDITORIAL WORK CALL WARREN DIRECTLY FAX MACHINE IN STUDIO

WARREN GEBERT • 12 STONEHAM LANE NEW CITY, N.Y. 10956 914-354-2536
R E P R E S E N T E D B Y
EILEEN MOSS & ASSOC. • 333 E. 49TH ST. N.Y. N.Y. 10017 212-980-8061
FOR EDITORIAL WORK CALL WARREN DIRECTLY FAX MACHINE IN STUDIO

PAMELA PATRICK

NANCY BRUCK

ARTIST REPRESENTATIVE

212 • 645 • 1547

B I L L   M A Y E R   I N C.

BILL MAYER 404–378-0686 FAX 404–373-1759 REPRESENTED BY THE WILLIAMS GROUP 404–873-2287 FAX 404–873-2280 IN NEW YORK TRICIA WEBER 212–768-0481 FAX 212–768-0079

D A V I D   M C K E L V E Y

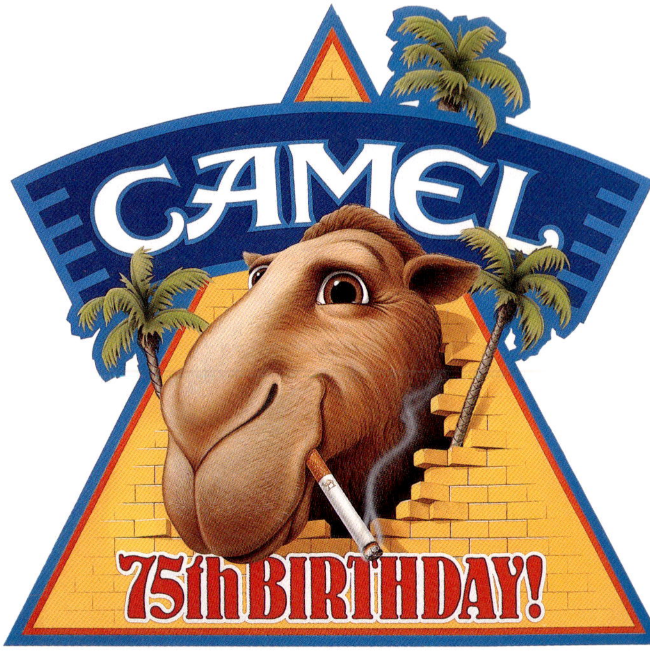

DAVID McKELVEY REPRESENTED BY ◆ THE WILLIAMS GROUP ◆ 404-873-2287 ◆ IN NEW YORK CONTACT TRICIA WEBER ◆ 212-768-0481

DANNY SMYTHE
ILLUSTRATIONS

REPRESENTED BY

THE
WILLIAMS
GROUP

404-873-2287

In New York
TRICIA WEBER
38 West 38 Street
New York, NY 10018
212-768-0481

Jim

S A L V A T I

818.441.2544

NEW YORK REPRESENTATIVE • TRICIA WEBER • THE WEBER GROUP • 212•768•0481

R I C K   L O V E L L

REPRESENTED BY ■ THE WILLIAMS GROUP ■ (404) 873-2287 ■ IN NEW YORK CONTACT TRICIA WEBER ■ (212) 768-0481

DANIEL SCHWARTZ

ANNUAL REPORT AMFAC CORP

THE CHICAGO DAILY NEWS

48 EAST 13TH STREET, NEW YORK, N.Y. 10003 (212) 533-0237

David Lesh

5693 N. Meridian Street
Indianapolis, IN 46208
1•317•253•3141

Represented by:
Joanne Palulian

18 McKinley Street
Rowayton, CT 06853

1•203•866•3734
1•212•581•8338

A.R.A. Services/Spiro & Assoc., Olympics.

Bob Ziering represents Bob Ziering (212) 873-0034

Poster/Tokyo City Keiba

Clients include: IBM, Exxon, Mobil, N.Y.C. Opera, DDB Needham, Simon & Schuster, Franklin Library, Newsweek, Esty, DMB&B, Walt Disney, Buntin, Rumrill-Hoyt, Cosmair, Liggett & Stashower, N.W. Ayer McCaffrey & McCall, McCann-Erickson, Channel 13, United Artists, NBC, ABC, CBS, Time, N.Y. Zoological Society, National Endowment For The Humanities. Corporate inquiries invited.

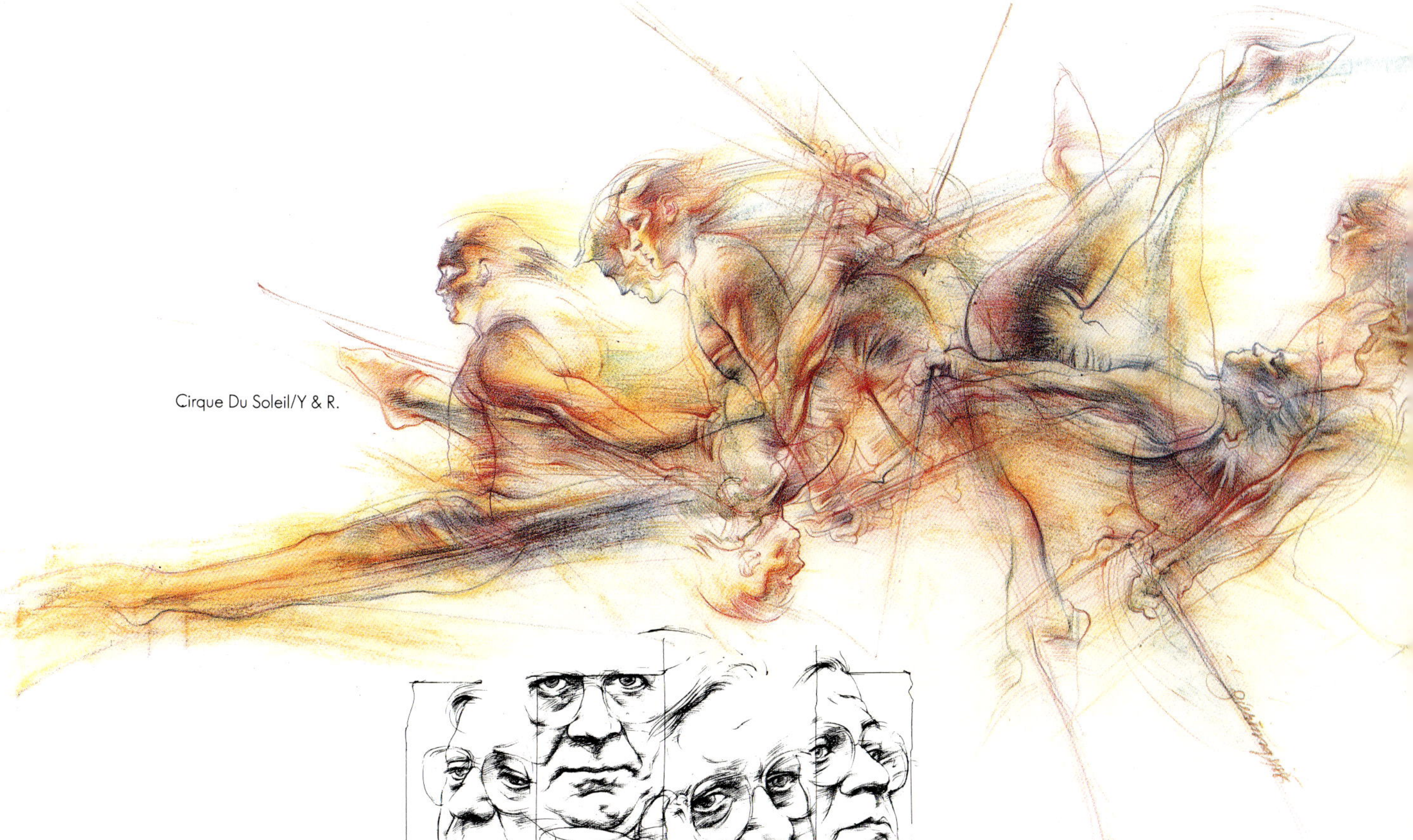

Cirque Du Soleil/Y & R.

Harvard Business Review.

Hakuhodo Inc., Tokyo.

Bob Ziering represents Bob Ziering (212) 873-0034

DOUGLAS FRASER

NORTHEAST STATES **212-929-5590** LINDGREN & SMITH
WEST & MIDWEST STATES **415-552-4252** JAN COLLIER

ROBERT GANTT STEELE

REPRESENTED BY
LINDGREN & SMITH (212) 929·5590 IN THE NORTHEAST
JAN COLLIER (415) 552·4252 OUTSIDE THE NORTHEAST

Jacqui Morgan

Chicago Tribune

JACQUI MORGAN STUDIO • 692 GREENWICH STREET • NEW YORK, NY 10014 • 212•463•8488

Paola Piglia

(212) 393-9207

28 Cliff St. #3
New York NY 10038

CIARDIELLO

Joe Ciardiello

2182 Clove Rd.

Staten Island, N.Y. 10305

(718) 727-4757

RAFAŁ OLBIŃSKI

BOWNE & CO. ANNUAL REPORT

REPUBLIC NEW YORK CORP. ANNUAL REPORT

CHIEF EXECUTIVE MAGAZINE

CONTINENTAL INSURANCE CORP. ANNUAL REPORT

represented by

T A N I A

TANIA KIMCHE ARTISTS REPRESENTATIVE 470 West 23rd St., N.Y. N.Y. 10011
(212) 242-6367

THEO RUDNAK
1151 WEST PEACHTREE STREET
ATLANTA, GEORGIA
30309/404.876.4058

RENARD REPRESENTS
212.490.2450

Min Jae Hong
310 East 23 Street, New York, New York 10010 (212) 674-4320

TERRY
ALLEN
718-727-0723
FAX 718-727-0927

Steve Dininno
258 Jefferson Ave. • Island Park, NY 11558 • (516) 431-1495 • Fax on premises

DANIEL
KIRK

85 SOUTH STREET 6 NORTH NEW YORK CITY 10038 212 825-0190

Business Week

Boston Globe

DEBORAH HEALY

72 WATCHUNG AVENUE

UPPER MONTCLAIR, NJ 07043

201 746 2549

Donald Sacks World Financial Center

J E A N - F R A N C O I S   P O D E V I N

2 1 2 / 9 6 4 - 4 2 4 4

GREG VOTH

231 WEST 20 NY, NY 10011 TEL. AND FAX (212) 807-9766

NEW YORK MAGAZINE, SPECIAL ADVERTISING SECTION

HARPER'S MAGAZINE

NEW YORK TIMES MAGAZINE

WAMSUTTA/PACIFIC

SELF PROMOTIONAL

MARK
FREDRICKSON
REPRESENTED BY
CECI BARTELS
ASSOCIATES
212 912 1877
314 241 9028
FAX

BOB PETERS

Represented by: GERALD & CULLEN RAPP, Inc.
108 E. 35th STREET(#3), NEW YORK, NY 10016
PHONE: 212-889-3337 FAX:212-889-3341

HUMOROUS ILLUSTRATION

Andy Levine

30-85 36th Street, #2
Astoria, N.Y. 11103
Fax In Studio

(718) 956-8539

Business Week

P.C. Computing

Changing Times

N.Y. Times

"Hey, We Ain't Laffin'!"
Z
BRRRP!
WHOOPEE CUSHION
Z
©1989 E.H. Smith
Why Not?
CARTOON
ART
THESE
DAYS
IS
TOO
HAPPY!
BAG 'O' LAFFS
Dark Humor comes easily to E.H. Smith in his semi-dark studio:
HELLO ~ I AM ELWOOD H. SMITH. LET'S MAKE 1990 THE "YEAR OF THE GROUCH"!
CALL MAGGIE!
MAGGIE PICKARD!
MAGGIE, HIS REP!
BAG ON LAMP
DRIBBLE GLASS
A WOOL SWEATER AND NO SHIRT KEEPS HIS SMILE WEAK.
SEE HOW HE DRAWS ME... I'M REALLY A CUTE BEAGLE!
ELWOOD BRINGS THE ENTIRE HOUSE DOWN!
CRUEL!
CAT
Really cute ideas are tossed out
So, if you need a little grumpiness out there, dial 914·876·2358 ★ 2 Locust Grove Rd., Rhinebeck, N.Y. 12572

GARY 'MAD DOG' BASEMAN

BITE THE HAND THAT FEEDS YOU

WORLD FAMOUS STUDIOS 443 12TH ST. BROOKLYN NY 11215
WG WISEGEIST AFFILIATE 718.499.9358 FAX. ANIMATION REEL.

INTERNATIONAL AWARD WINNING SATIRIC ARTIST
BILL LEE 792 COLUMBUS AVENUE (1-O)
NEW YORK CITY 10025/(212) 866-5664

*(animals also availab

DEBRA SOLOMON

536 WEST 111TH STREET APT. 55, N.Y., N.Y. 10025 (212) 662-5619 • FAX: (212) 866-8547

CLIENTS INCLUDE: IBM • AMERICAN EXPRESS • PRUDENTIAL • PROCTER & GAMBLE UNION CARBIDE • NEW YORK TIMES • VOGUE • GLAMOUR • HALLMARK • RANDOM HOUSE NEW AMERICAN LIBRARY • PUTNAM • SIMON & SCHUSTER • BANTAM • WORKMAN PRESS

Animation Reel On Request

J E F F   S E A V E R

JEFF SEAVER 130 W 24TH ST #4B NY, NY 10011-1906 FAX 212/255-3823 PHONE 212/741-2279

SCHEUER

PHILIP A. SCHEUER/ILLUSTRATION
126 FIFTH AVENUE, NEW YORK, NY 10011
212·620·0728

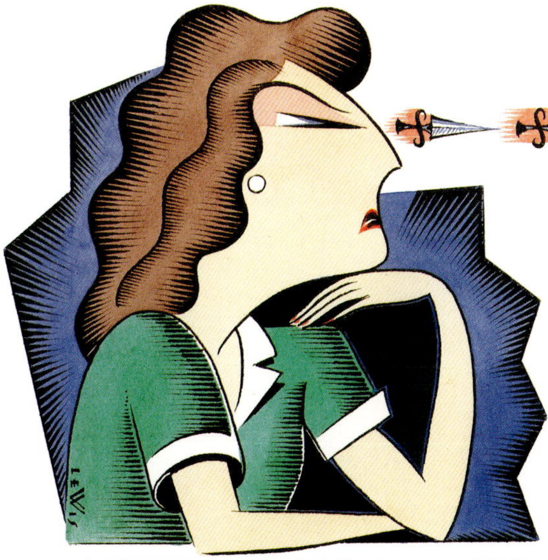

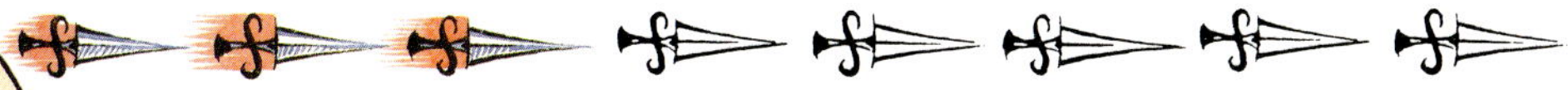

TIM LEWIS

184 ST. JOHNS PLACE
BROOKLYN, NY, 11217
718/857-3406

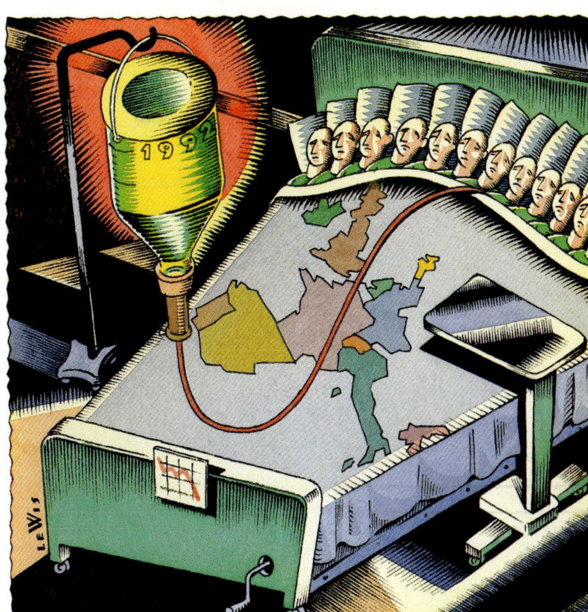

"Illustration in the Grand Tradition"

Tim Raglin

REPRESENTED BY PAT LINDGREN & PIPER SMITH 212-929-5590

LINDGREN & SMITH

HUMOR.

PATRICK McDONNELL ~ 201·549·9341 ·FAX·201·548·4986

WHITTLE COMMUNICATIONS

NELLE DAVIS

20 East 17 New York, NY 10003 212·807·7737

THE NEW YORK TIMES

7 DAYS

PETER DE SÈVE 25 PARK PLACE BROOKLYN NEW YORK 11217 ANIMATION REEL AVAILABLE 718 398 8099

TWILIGHT ZONE

BIG JOE TURNER: MTV TO GO

RANDY JONES

323 EAST 10th STREET
NEW YORK, N.Y. 10009
(212) 677-5387
FAX AVAILABLE

NEWSWEEK INTERNATIONAL

B o n n i e T i m m o n s

(215) 247-3556 FAX (215) 242-4957

Represented by
IMPRESS: ART
(212) 787-1340

Clients include: Time, Newsweek, U.S. News, New York Times, Washington Post, American Express, ITT, 911 Emergency Network

DAVID CATROW

ILLUSTRATION • INSPIRATION

212-627-7058

KAREN LEON

154-01 BARCLAY AVENUE, FLUSHING, N.Y. 11355 (718) 461-2050, (718) 463-3159.

ILLUSTRATION, HUMOR & EDITORIAL CARTOONS, CARICATURES.

CLIENTS: AMERICAN EXPRESS, KELLOGG'S, SEAGRAM'S, CRAIN'S NEW YORK BUSINESS, WOMAN'S WORLD, THOMAS PUBLISHING CO., OPPENHEIMER & CO., FIRST MAGAZINE, PUBLIC RELATIONS SOCIETY OF AMERICA, BOOK-OF-THE-MONTH CLUB, EQUITABLE LIFE INSURANCE CO.

Russell O. Jones
199 Eighth Avenue, Apt. C4
Brooklyn, NY 11215
(718) 965-3224

S.I. International
43 East 19th Street
New York, New York 10003
(212) 254-4996

Dr. Herb Spiers
Illustration Specialist

Representing:

Steve Haefele

LETTERING & DESIGN

B I N I A S Z

BINIASZ GRAPHIC DESIGN • ILLUSTRATION
57 JANE ST., NEW YORK, NEW YORK 10014
LOGOS BROCHURES POSTERS PACKAGING
CORPORATE IDENTITY AND ILLUSTRATION
TEL. 212 979-0025 FAX 212 727-2778

JON VALK
GRAPHIC DESIGN
245 E. 24 STREET · NEW YORK · NY · 10010
212 · 889 · 4490

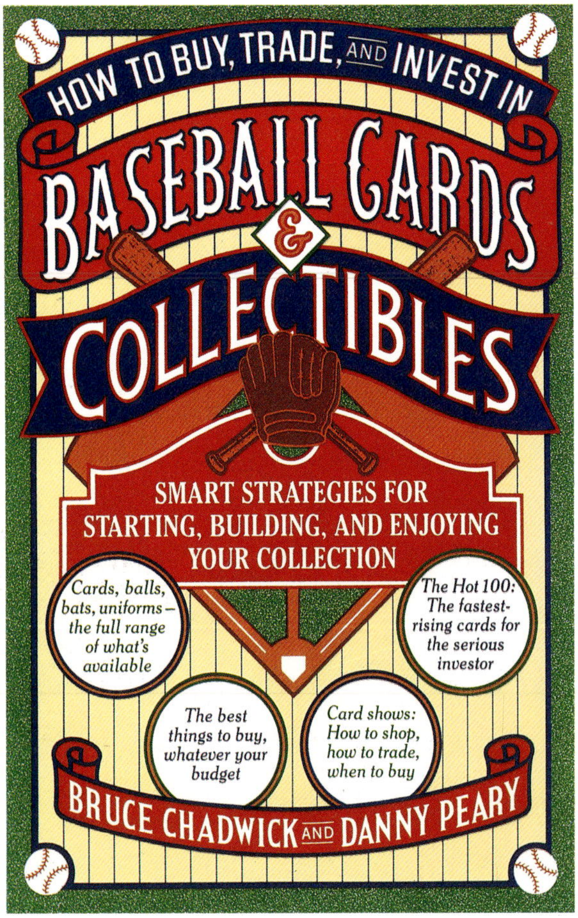

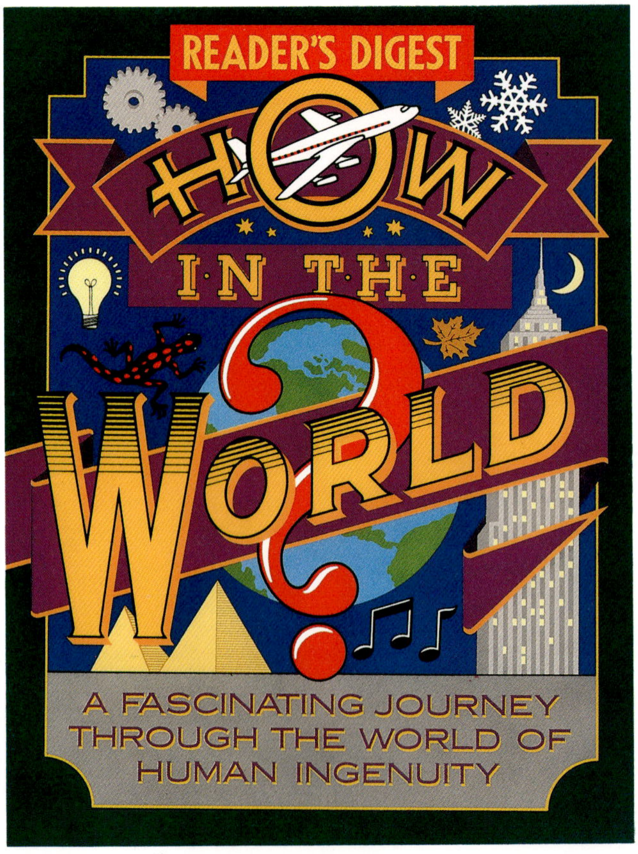

John Stevens DESIGN

PHONE
516-579-5352
FAX
516-735-6535

LOGOS • LETTERING
TYPE DESIGN &
CALLIGRAPHY

CHEMICAL BANK Gold CREDIT ON DEMAND

BANGKOK

HBO Showcase

Anita Baker

THE CARE OF BRASS

Movin Up to 7 Seven Up

GRANDE ILLUSION

Macy's Flower Show 1989

THE FOUR DAY REVOLUTION

wide style

Lon Po Po
A RED-RIDING HOOD STORY FROM CHINA

The TWICE Registry of Leading Consumer Electronics Video Software Retailers

AB BB

Made for each other

HOME FURNISHING & INTERIOR DESIGN SHOW

The Cafe

Puro Color

BABYTALK

All For One One For All

WOODBURY COMMON
THE UNCOMMON SHOPPING EXPERIENCE

COCKTAILS•FOR•50

Calligraphy

Lettering

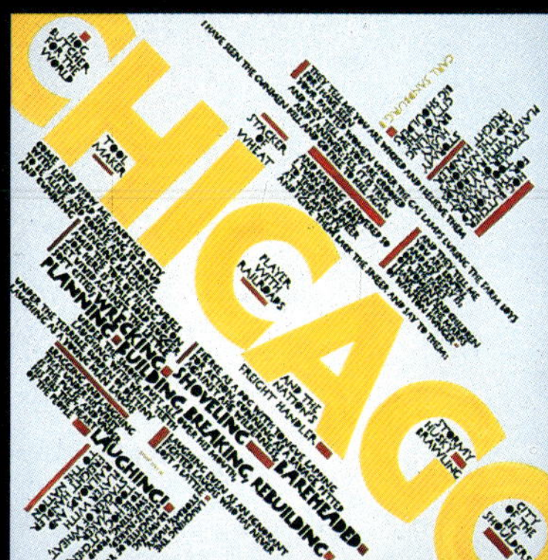

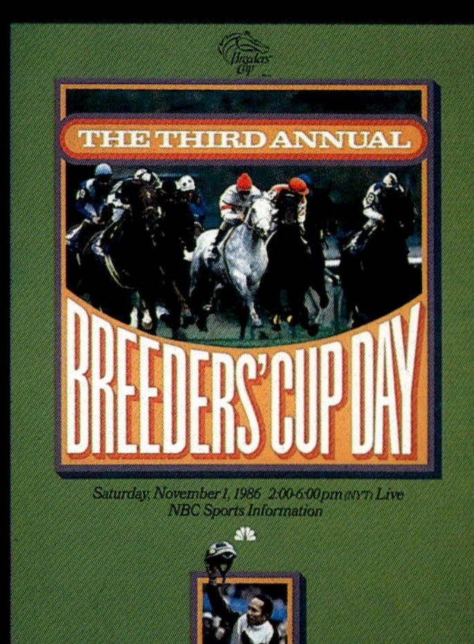

Design

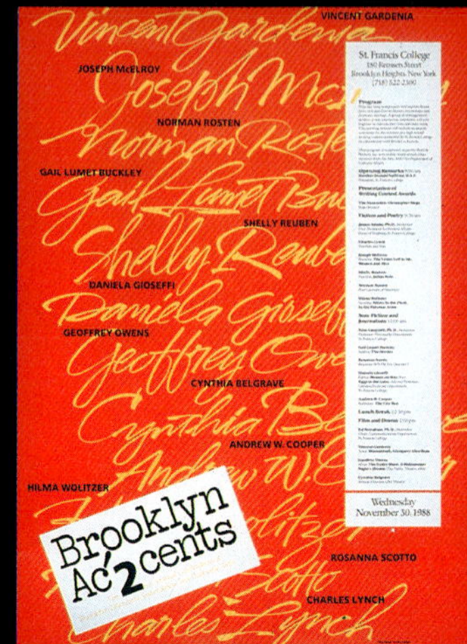

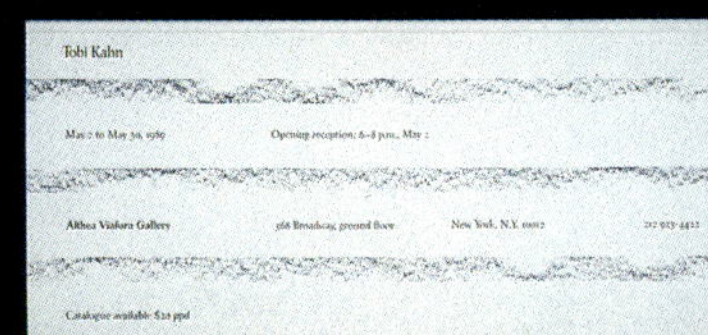

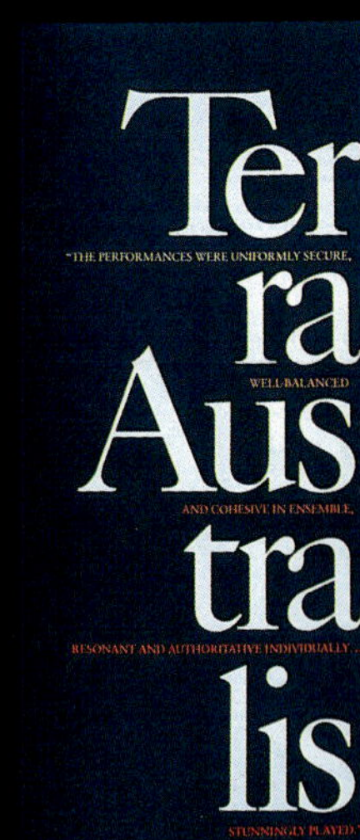

Paul Shaw / Letter Design · 785 West End Avenue · New York City 10025 · 212 / 666-3738

WORLD
PEACE
"SALSA"
PEÑA
PARFUM
Ardiénte
DE NUEVA YORK
Avon Color
Misha
RAYMOND HERNANDEZ DESIGN
718•462•9072
DESIGN, LETTERING, ILLUSTRATION
STOCK COLLECTION OF PATTERN DESIGNS
CALL FOR APPOINTMENT TO PREVIEW COLLECTIONS
© RAYMOND HERNANDEZ 1990

STEPHEN FO

GOING PLACES

THE WORLD OF
SCIENCE FICTION

BOOKS OF
MYSTERY & CRIME

BURKE & BURKE

GRAPHIC DESIGN A

STER › DESIGN

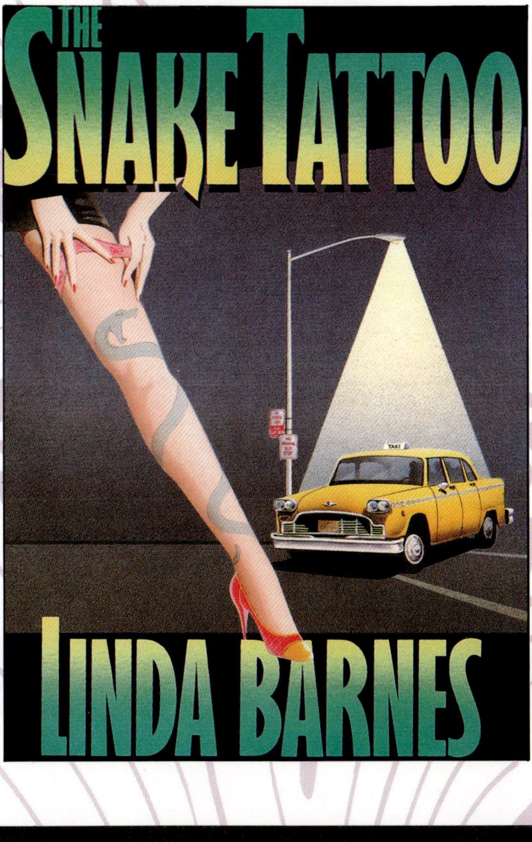

145 WEST 28 ST · NYC
212.967.2533
FAX: 212.947.3253

A UNIQUE BLEND
OF DESIGN
LETTERING AND
ILLUSTRATION
FOR AD AGENCIES
CORPORATIONS
AND PUBLISHERS

DESIGNERS
STEPHEN FOSTER
LISA VALENTI

ND ILLUSTRATION

Paul Perlow Design
212•758•4358
Fine Typography & Lettering
Graphic Images & Trademarks
Represented in Paris, France:
Hugo Weinberg Associés
1-4 266 6200

LETTERING ART & DESIGN

Partial Client List:
CBS Records International
Prentice Hall/JC Penney
NY Times/Reader's Digest
Polygram Records/SSC&B
Saatchi, Saatchi, & Compton
Business Week, Family Circle

MASTER COMP

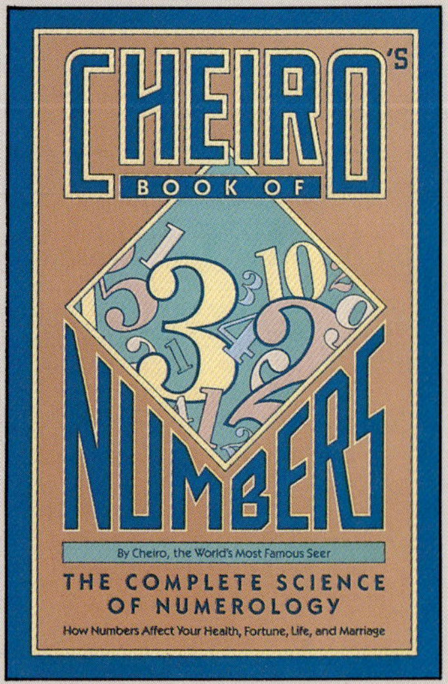

GENESIS

BusinessWeek
INTERNATIONAL BusinessWeek

PAUL PERLOW DESIGN • 123 EAST 54TH ST. • NEW YORK, NY 10022 • 212 • 758 • 4358

Thirty East 21st Street, New York City 10010
(212) 777-1500

303 Park Avenue South, New York City 10010
(212) 674-1185

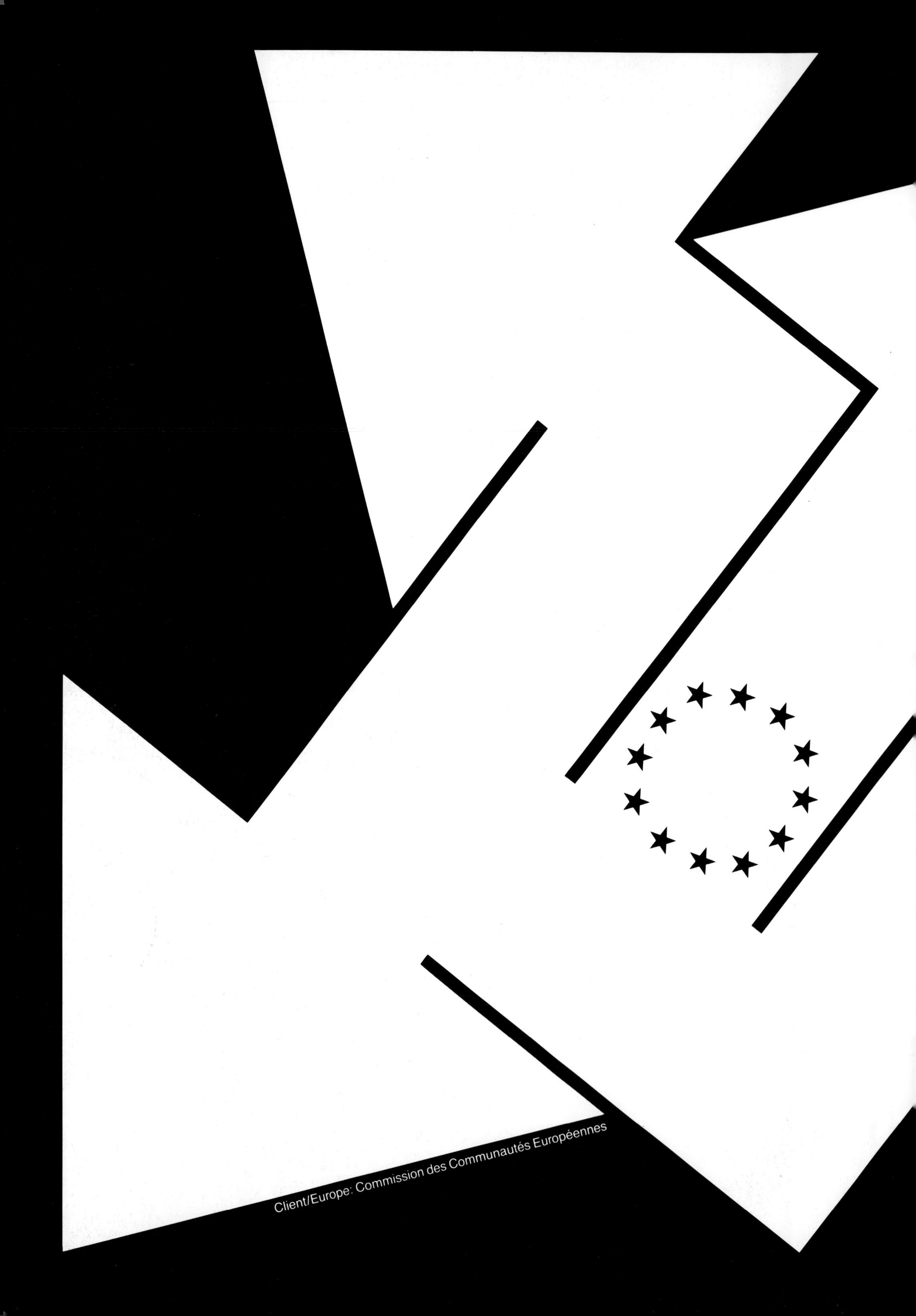
Client/Europe: Commission des Communautés Européennes

Client/The José Limón Dance Company
STUDIO 54
Client/Studio 54
Client/The Equus Company
GILBERT LESSER INCR INC.
Gilbert Lesser
Inter National
Creative Resources Inc.
Suite 43.38
1271 Avenue of the Americas
Rockefeller Center
New York, New York 10020
212.522.8400
CGSA
38 rue Croix
de Petits Champs
75001 Paris
42.61.81.06

B Y H A N D D E S I G N

By Hand Design
Art direction, graphic design, typography and lettering with a human touch. Logos, packaging, catalogs, brochures, book titles, editorial covers, pages or formats. Concept to final art. Photo studio on premises.

Clients include:
Arista Records, Bloomingdale's, Clairol, Commart, FOX/MMJ Direct, Gourmet Retailer Magazine, Kallir/Philips/Ross, Macy's, Marke Communications, Met Life, Metro, New American Library, People Magazine, Promotion Dynamics, Random House, Robert Lee Morris, Warner Books.

SHERRY FREDY
STUDIO: (212) 627-1867
111 W 24 ST., NYC

Enjoy

METRO

bloomingdale's GOLD LINE DOUBLE CHOCOLATE CHIP COOKIES

BLOOMINGDALE'S

ROBERT LEE MORRIS

Feel the Difference

CLAIROL

Aretha Franklin Through the Storm

ARISTA RECORDS

METRO

LULU CARDS

STILLWATER ASSOCIATES PICK-OF-THE-HUNT LIMITED

the People weekly family

type design

BY HAND DESIGN